Blue Ocean Classics

W. CHAN KIM
RENÉE MAUBORGNE

HARVARD BUSINESS REVIEW PRESS

BOSTON, MASSACHUSETTS

Copyright 2019 Harvard Business School Publishing Corporation
Originally published in *Harvard Business Review* in October 2004,
May 2014, and March 2015
Reprint #R0410D, #10104, #10103
All rights reserved

Printed in the United States of America

10 9 8 7 6 5 4 3 2 1

The web addresses referenced in this book were live and correct at the time of the book's publication but may be subject to change.

Library of Congress Cataloging-in-Publication data is forthcoming.

ISBN: 978-1-63369-737-9
eISBN: 978-1-63369-738-6

The paper used in this publication meets the requirements of the American National Standard for Permanence of Paper for Publications and Documents in Libraries and Archives Z39.48-1992.

CONTENTS

PREFACE

Blue ocean strategy is one of the most influential business ideas of our time. The award-winning eponymous book by world-renowned thought leaders W. Chan Kim and Renée Mauborgne has become a global phenomenon that changed the language of business forever. First published in 2005 and reissued in an expanded edition in 2015, *Blue Ocean Strategy* has sold over 3.6 million copies, is a bestseller across five continents, and is available in forty-six languages. The *Financial Times* recognized it as "one of the bestselling business books of the century."

This collection of three classic *Harvard Business Review* articles by Kim and Mauborgne provides readers with a concise introduction to the theory of blue ocean strategy, its central tenets and practical insights.

In "Blue Ocean Strategy," the first article to unveil the idea and coin the term, Kim and Mauborgne reveal their red ocean versus blue ocean strategy framework. Bringing together the research findings, underlying concepts, and unique logic that forms the basis of their theory, Kim and Mauborgne explain the key differences between market-competing and market-creating strategy, describe what is and what isn't a blue ocean strategy, and show you how to apply blue ocean strategic moves.

After analyzing blue ocean successes and failures for more than a decade, Kim and Mauborgne identified a common factor that seems to consistently undermine the execution of market-creating strategies—the mental models of the managers involved in them. In their research, the authors encountered six traps that effectively keep managers anchored in red oceans and prevent them from entering blue oceans of uncontested market space. "Red Ocean Traps" looks at each trap in detail and helps managers avoid getting caught in them.

Because blue ocean strategies create new market space, they have the potential to inspire and reenergize your company's talent. But many managers lack a clear understanding of what it would take to unlock the ocean of unrealized talent hidden in their organizations in order to achieve high impact. The article "Blue Ocean Leadership" uses the core concepts and tools of blue ocean strategy to look not only at what leaders actually do but also at which acts and activities they could do differently to boost people's motivation as well as their business results. Designed to be used at all levels—top, middle, and frontline—the tools in this article extend the organization's leadership capabilities and unleash its previously unexploited talent and energy.

As you will learn—or rediscover—in these classic articles, formulating a blue ocean strategy is ultimately a creative act. It's about seeing your world differently and unleashing the creativity of the people in your organization. This collection of articles is the ideal start for creating more blue oceans.

Blue Ocean Strategy

A onetime accordion player, stilt walker, and fire-eater, Guy Laliberté is now CEO of one of Canada's largest cultural exports, Cirque du Soleil. Founded in 1984 by a group of street performers, Cirque has staged dozens of productions seen by some 40 million people in 90 cities around the world. In 20 years, Cirque has achieved revenues that Ringling Bros. and Barnum & Bailey—the world's leading circus—took more than a century to attain.

Cirque's rapid growth occurred in an unlikely setting. The circus business was (and still is) in long-term decline. Alternative forms of entertainment—sporting events, TV, and video games—were casting a growing shadow. Children, the mainstay of the circus audience, preferred PlayStations to circus acts. There was also rising sentiment, fueled by animal rights groups, against the use of animals, traditionally an integral part of the circus. On the supply side, the star performers that Ringling and the other circuses relied on to draw in the crowds could often name their own terms. As a result, the industry was hit by steadily decreasing audiences and increasing costs. What's more, any new entrant to this business would be competing against a formidable incumbent that for most of the last century had set the industry standard.

How did Cirque profitably increase revenues by a factor of 22 over the last ten years in such an unattractive environment? The tagline for one of the first Cirque productions is revealing: "We reinvent the circus." Cirque did not make its money by competing within the confines of the existing industry or by stealing customers from Ringling and the others. Instead it created uncontested market space that made the competition irrelevant. It pulled in a whole new group of customers who were traditionally noncustomers of the industry—adults and corporate clients who had turned to theater, opera, or ballet and were, therefore, prepared to pay several times more than the price of a conventional circus ticket for an unprecedented entertainment experience.

To understand the nature of Cirque's achievement, you have to realize that the business universe consists of two distinct kinds of space, which we think of as red and blue oceans. Red oceans represent all the industries in existence today—the known market space. In red oceans, industry boundaries are defined and accepted, and the competitive rules of the game are well understood. Here, companies try to outperform their rivals in order to grab a greater share of existing demand. As the space gets more and more crowded, prospects for profits and growth are reduced. Products turn into commodities, and increasing competition turns the water bloody.

Blue oceans denote all the industries *not* in existence today—the unknown market space, untainted by competition. In blue oceans, demand is created rather than fought over. There is ample opportunity for growth that is both profitable and rapid. There are two ways to create blue oceans. In a few cases, companies can give rise to completely new industries, as eBay did with the online auction industry. But in most cases, a blue ocean is created from within a red ocean when a company alters the boundaries of an existing industry. As will become evident later, this is what Cirque did. In breaking through the boundary traditionally separating circus and theater, it made a new and profitable blue ocean from within the red ocean of the circus industry.

Cirque is just one of more than 150 blue ocean creations that we have studied in over 30 industries, using data stretching back more than 100 years. We analyzed companies that created those blue oceans and their less successful competitors, which were caught in red oceans. In studying these data, we have observed a consistent pattern of strategic thinking behind the creation of new markets and industries, what we call blue ocean strategy. The logic behind blue ocean strategy parts with traditional models focused on competing in existing market space. Indeed, it can be argued that managers' failure to realize the differences between red and blue ocean strategy lies behind the difficulties many companies encounter as they try to break from the competition.

In this article, we present the concept of blue ocean strategy and describe its defining characteristics. We assess the profit and growth consequences of blue oceans and discuss why their creation is a rising imperative for companies in the future. We believe that an understanding of blue ocean strategy will help today's companies as they struggle to thrive in an accelerating and expanding business universe.

BLUE AND RED OCEANS

Although the term may be new, blue oceans have always been with us. Look back 100 years and ask yourself which industries known today were then unknown. The answer: Industries as basic as automobiles, music recording, aviation, petrochemicals, pharmaceuticals, and management consulting were unheard-of or had just begun to emerge. Now turn the clock back only 30 years and ask yourself the same question. Again, a plethora of multibillion-dollar industries jump out: mutual funds, cellular telephones, biotechnology, discount retailing, express package delivery, snowboards, coffee bars, and home videos, to name a few. Just three decades ago, none of these industries existed in a meaningful way.

This time, put the clock forward 20 years. Ask yourself: How many industries that are unknown today will exist then? If history is any predictor of the future, the answer is many. Companies have a huge capacity to create new industries and re-create existing ones, a fact that is reflected in the deep changes that have been necessary in the way industries are classified. The half-century-old Standard Industrial Classification (SIC) system was replaced in 1997 by the North American Industry Classification System (NAICS). The new system expanded the ten SIC industry sectors into 20 to reflect the emerging realities of new industry territories—blue oceans.

The services sector under the old system, for example, is now seven sectors ranging from information to health care and social assistance. Given that these classification systems are designed for standardization and continuity, such a replacement shows how significant a source of economic growth the creation of blue oceans has been.

Looking forward, it seems clear to us that blue oceans will remain the engine of growth. Prospects in most established market spaces—red oceans—are shrinking steadily. Technological advances have substantially improved industrial productivity, permitting suppliers to produce an unprecedented array of products and services. And as trade barriers between nations and regions fall and information on products and prices becomes instantly and globally available, niche markets and monopoly havens are continuing to disappear. At the same time, there is little evidence of any increase in demand, at least in the developed markets, where recent United Nations statistics even point to declining populations. The result is that in more and more industries, supply is overtaking demand.

This situation has inevitably hastened the commoditization of products and services, stoked price wars, and shrunk profit margins. According to recent studies, major American brands in a variety of product and service categories have become more and more alike. And as brands become more similar, people increasingly base purchase choices on price. People no longer insist, as in the past, that their laundry detergent be Tide. Nor do they necessarily stick to Colgate when there is a special promotion for Crest, and vice versa. In overcrowded industries, differentiating brands becomes harder both in economic upturns and in downturns.

THE PARADOX OF STRATEGY

Unfortunately, most companies seem becalmed in their red oceans. In a study of business launches in 108 companies, we found that 86% of those new ventures were line extensions—incremental improvements to existing industry offerings—and a mere 14% were aimed at creating new markets or industries. While line extensions did account for 62% of the total revenues, they delivered only 39% of the total profits. By contrast, the 14% invested in creating new markets and industries delivered 38% of total revenues and a startling 61% of total profits.

So why the dramatic imbalance in favor of red oceans? Part of the explanation is that corporate strategy is heavily influenced by its roots in military strategy. The very language of strategy is deeply imbued with military references—chief executive "officers" in "headquarters," "troops" on the "front lines." Described this way, strategy is all about red ocean competition. It is about confronting an opponent and driving him off a battlefield of limited territory. Blue ocean strategy, by contrast, is about doing business where there is no competitor. It is about creating new land, not dividing up existing land. Focusing on the red ocean therefore means accepting the key constraining factors of war—limited terrain and the need to beat an enemy to succeed. And it means denying the distinctive strength of the business world—the capacity to create new market space that is uncontested.

The tendency of corporate strategy to focus on winning against rivals was exacerbated by the meteoric rise of Japanese companies in the 1970s and 1980s. For the first time in corporate history, customers were deserting Western companies in droves. As competition mounted in the global marketplace, a slew of red ocean strategies emerged, all arguing that competition was at the core of corporate success and failure. Today, one hardly talks about strategy without using the language of competition. The term that best symbolizes this is "competitive advantage." In the competitive-advantage worldview, companies are often driven to outperform rivals and capture greater shares of existing market space.

Of course competition matters. But by focusing on competition, scholars, companies, and consultants have ignored two very important—and, we would argue, far more lucrative—aspects of strategy: One is to find and develop markets where there is little or no competition—blue oceans—and the other is to exploit and protect blue oceans. These challenges are very different from those to which strategists have devoted most of their attention.

TOWARD BLUE OCEAN STRATEGY

What kind of strategic logic is needed to guide the creation of blue oceans? To answer that question, we looked back over 100 years of data on blue ocean creation to see what patterns could be discerned. Some of our data are presented in the table "A snapshot of blue ocean creation" at the end of this article. It shows an overview of key blue ocean creations in three industries that closely touch people's lives: autos—how people get to work; computers—what people use at work; and movie theaters—where people go after work for enjoyment. We found that:

Blue oceans are not about technology innovation

Leading-edge technology is sometimes involved in the creation of blue oceans, but it is not a defining feature of them. This is often true even in industries that are technology intensive. As the table reveals, across all three representative industries, blue oceans were seldom the result of technological innovation per se; the underlying

technology was often already in existence.
Even Ford's revolutionary assembly line
can be traced to the meatpacking industry in America. Like those within the auto
industry, the blue oceans within the computer industry did not come about through
technology innovations alone but by linking
technology to what buyers valued. As with
the IBM 650 and the Compaq PC server, this
often involved simplifying the technology.

*Incumbents often create blue oceans—and
usually within their core businesses*

GM, the Japanese automakers, and Chrysler
were established players when they created
blue oceans in the auto industry. So were
CTR and its later incarnation, IBM, and

Compaq in the computer industry. And in the cinema industry, the same can be said of palace theaters and AMC. Of the companies listed here, only Ford, Apple, Dell, and Nickelodeon were new entrants in their industries; the first three were start-ups, and the fourth was an established player entering an industry that was new to it. This suggests that incumbents are not at a disadvantage in creating new market spaces. Moreover, the blue oceans made by incumbents were usually within their core businesses. In fact, as the table shows, most blue oceans are created from within, not beyond, red oceans of existing industries. This challenges the view that new markets are in distant waters. Blue oceans are right next to you in every industry.

Company and industry are the wrong units of analysis

The traditional units of strategic analysis—company and industry—have little explanatory power when it comes to analyzing how and why blue oceans are created. There is no consistently excellent company; the same company can be brilliant at one time and wrongheaded at another. Every company rises and falls over time. Likewise, there is no perpetually excellent industry; relative attractiveness is driven largely by the creation of blue oceans from within them.

The most appropriate unit of analysis for explaining the creation of blue oceans is the strategic move—the set of managerial actions and decisions involved in making a major market-creating business offering. Compaq, for example, is considered by many people to be "unsuccessful" because it was acquired by Hewlett-Packard in 2001 and ceased to be a company. But the firm's ultimate fate does not invalidate the smart strategic move Compaq made that led to the creation of the multibillion-dollar market in PC servers, a move that was a key cause of the company's powerful comeback in the 1990s.

Creating blue oceans builds brands

So powerful is blue ocean strategy that a blue ocean strategic move can create brand equity that lasts for decades. Almost all of the companies listed in the table are remembered in no small part for the blue oceans they created long ago. Very few people alive today were around when the first Model T rolled off Henry Ford's assembly line in 1908, but the company's brand still benefits from that blue ocean move. IBM, too, is often regarded as an "American institution" largely for the blue oceans it created in computing; the 360 series was its equivalent of the Model T.

Our findings are encouraging for executives at the large, established corporations that are traditionally seen as the victims of new market space creation. For what they reveal is that large R&D budgets are not the key to creating new market space. The key is making the right strategic moves. What's more, companies that understand what drives a good strategic move will be well placed to create multiple blue oceans over time, thereby continuing to deliver high growth and profits over a sustained period. The creation of blue oceans, in other words, is a product of strategy and as such is very much a product of managerial action.

THE DEFINING CHARACTERISTICS

Our research shows several common characteristics across strategic moves that create blue oceans. We found that the creators of blue oceans, in sharp contrast to companies playing by traditional rules, never use the competition as a benchmark. Instead they make it irrelevant by creating a leap in value for both buyers and the company itself.

(The table "Red ocean versus blue ocean strategy" at the end of this article compares the chief characteristics of these two strategy models.)

Perhaps the most important feature of blue ocean strategy is that it rejects the fundamental tenet of conventional strategy: that a trade-off exists between value and cost. According to this thesis, companies can either create greater value for customers at a higher cost or create reasonable value at a lower cost. In other words, strategy is essentially a choice between differentiation and low cost. But when it comes to creating blue oceans, the evidence shows that successful companies pursue differentiation and low cost simultaneously.

To see how this is done, let us go back to Cirque du Soleil. At the time of Cirque's debut, circuses focused on benchmarking one another and maximizing their shares of shrinking demand by tweaking traditional circus acts. This included trying to secure more and better-known clowns and lion tamers, efforts that raised circuses' cost structure without substantially altering the circus experience. The result was rising costs without rising revenues and a downward spiral in overall circus demand. Enter Cirque. Instead of following the conventional logic of outpacing the competition by offering a better solution to the given problem—creating a circus with even greater fun and thrills—it redefined the problem itself by offering people the fun and thrill of the circus *and* the intellectual sophistication and artistic richness of the theater.

In designing performances that landed both these punches, Cirque had to reevaluate the components of the traditional circus offering. What the company found was that many of the elements considered essential to the fun and thrill of the circus were unnecessary and in many cases costly. For instance, most circuses offer animal acts. These are a heavy economic burden, because circuses have to shell out not only for the animals but also for their training, medical care, housing, insurance, and transportation. Yet Cirque found that the appetite for animal shows was rapidly diminishing because of rising public concern about the treatment of circus animals and the ethics of exhibiting them.

Similarly, although traditional circuses promoted their performers as stars, Cirque realized that the public no longer thought of circus artists as stars, at least not in the movie star sense. Cirque did away with traditional three-ring shows, too. Not only did these create confusion among spectators forced to switch their attention from one ring to another, they also increased the number of performers needed, with obvious cost implications. And while aisle concession sales appeared to be a good way to generate revenue, the high prices discouraged parents from making purchases and made them feel they were being taken for a ride.

Cirque found that the lasting allure of the traditional circus came down to just three factors: the clowns, the tent, and the classic acrobatic acts. So Cirque kept the clowns, while shifting their humor away from slapstick to a more enchanting, sophisticated style. It glamorized the tent, which many circuses had abandoned in favor of rented venues. Realizing that the tent, more than anything else, captured the magic of the circus, Cirque designed this classic symbol with a glorious external finish and a high level of audience comfort. Gone were the sawdust and hard benches. Acrobats and other thrilling performers were retained, but Cirque reduced their roles and made their acts more elegant by adding artistic flair.

Even as Cirque stripped away some of the traditional circus offerings, it injected new elements drawn from the world of theater. For instance, unlike traditional circuses featuring a series of unrelated acts, each Cirque creation resembles a theater performance in that it has a theme and story line. Although the themes are intentionally vague, they bring harmony and an intellectual element to the acts. Cirque also borrows ideas from Broadway. For example, rather than putting on the traditional "once and for all" show, Cirque mounts multiple productions based on different themes and story lines. As with Broadway productions, too, each Cirque show has an original musical score, which drives the performance, lighting, and timing of the acts, rather than the other way around. The productions feature abstract and spiritual dance, an idea derived from theater and ballet. By introducing these factors, Cirque has created highly sophisticated entertainments. And by staging multiple productions, Cirque gives people reason to come to the circus more often, thereby increasing revenues.

Cirque offers the best of both circus and theater. And by eliminating many of the most expensive elements of the circus, it has been able to dramatically reduce its cost structure, achieving both differentiation and low cost. (For a depiction of the economics underpinning blue ocean strategy, see the exhibit

"The simultaneous pursuit of differentiation and low cost" at the end of this article.)

By driving down costs while simultaneously driving up value for buyers, a company can achieve a leap in value for both itself and its customers. Since buyer value comes from the utility and price a company offers, and a company generates value for itself through cost structure and price, blue ocean strategy is achieved only when the whole system of a company's utility, price, and cost activities is properly aligned. It is this whole-system approach that makes the creation of blue oceans a sustainable strategy. Blue ocean strategy integrates the range of a firm's functional and operational activities.

A rejection of the trade-off between low cost and differentiation implies a fundamental change in strategic mind-set—we cannot emphasize enough how fundamental a shift it is. The red ocean assumption that industry structural conditions are a given and firms are forced to compete within them is based on an intellectual worldview that academics call the *structuralist* view, or *environmental determinism*. According to this view, companies and managers are largely at the mercy of economic forces greater than themselves. Blue ocean strategies, by contrast, are based on a worldview in which market boundaries and industries can be reconstructed by the actions and beliefs of industry players. We call this the *reconstructionist* view.

The founders of Cirque du Soleil clearly did not feel constrained to act within the confines of their industry. Indeed, is Cirque really a circus with all that it has eliminated, reduced, raised, and created? Or is it theater? If it is theater, then what genre—Broadway show, opera, ballet? The magic of Cirque was created through a reconstruction of elements drawn from all of these alternatives. In the end, Cirque is none of them and a little of all of them. From within the red oceans of theater and circus, Cirque has created a blue ocean of uncontested market space that has, as yet, no name.

BARRIERS TO IMITATION

Companies that create blue oceans usually reap the benefits without credible challenges for ten to 15 years, as was the case with Cirque du Soleil, Home Depot, Federal Express, Southwest Airlines, and CNN, to name just a few. The reason is that blue ocean strategy creates considerable economic and cognitive barriers to imitation.

For a start, adopting a blue ocean creator's business model is easier to imagine than to do. Because blue ocean creators immediately attract customers in large volumes, they are able to generate scale economies very rapidly, putting would-be imitators at an immediate and continuing cost disadvantage. The huge economies of scale in purchasing that Wal-Mart enjoys, for example, have significantly discouraged other companies from imitating its business model. The immediate attraction of large numbers of customers can also create network externalities. The more customers eBay has online, the more attractive the auction site becomes for both sellers and buyers of wares, giving users few incentives to go elsewhere.

When imitation requires companies to make changes to their whole system of activities, organizational politics may impede a would-be competitor's ability to switch to the divergent business model of a blue ocean strategy. For instance, airlines trying to follow Southwest's example of offering the speed of air travel with the flexibility and cost of driving would have faced major revisions in routing, training, marketing, and pricing, not to mention culture. Few established airlines had the flexibility to make such extensive organizational and operating changes overnight. Imitating a whole-system approach is not an easy feat.

The cognitive barriers can be just as effective. When a company offers a leap in value, it rapidly earns brand buzz and a loyal following in the marketplace. Experience shows that even the most expensive marketing campaigns struggle to unseat a blue ocean creator. Microsoft, for example, has been trying for more than ten years to occupy the center of the blue ocean that Intuit created with its financial software product Quicken. Despite all of its efforts and all of its investment, Microsoft has not been able to unseat Intuit as the industry leader.

In other situations, attempts to imitate a blue ocean creator conflict with the imitator's existing brand image. The Body Shop, for example, shuns top models and makes no promises of eternal youth and beauty. For the established cosmetic brands like Estée Lauder and L'Oréal, imitation was very difficult, because it would have signaled a complete invalidation of their current images, which are based on promises of eternal youth and beauty.

A CONSISTENT PATTERN

While our conceptual articulation of the pattern may be new, blue ocean strategy has always existed, whether or not companies have been conscious of the fact. Just consider the striking parallels between the Cirque du Soleil theater-circus experience and Ford's creation of the Model T.

At the end of the nineteenth century, the automobile industry was small and unattractive. More than 500 automakers in America competed in turning out handmade luxury cars that cost around $1,500 and were enormously *un*popular with all but the very rich. Anticar activists tore up roads, ringed parked cars with barbed wire, and organized boycotts of car-driving businessmen and politicians. Woodrow Wilson caught the spirit of the times when he said in 1906 that "nothing has spread socialistic feeling more than the automobile." He called it "a picture of the arrogance of wealth."

Instead of trying to beat the competition and steal a share of existing demand from other automakers, Ford reconstructed the industry boundaries of cars and horse-drawn carriages to create a blue ocean. At the time, horse-drawn carriages were the primary means of local transportation across America. The carriage had two distinct advantages over cars. Horses could easily negotiate the bumps and mud that stymied cars—especially in rain and snow—on the nation's ubiquitous dirt roads. And horses and carriages were much easier to maintain than the luxurious autos of the time, which frequently broke down, requiring expert repairmen who were expensive and in short supply. It was Henry Ford's understanding of these advantages that showed him how he could break away from the competition and unlock enormous untapped demand.

Ford called the Model T the car "for the great multitude, constructed of the best materials." Like Cirque, the Ford Motor Company made the competition irrelevant. Instead of creating fashionable, customized cars for weekends in the countryside, a luxury few could justify, Ford built a car that, like the horse-drawn carriage, was for everyday use. The Model T came in just one color, black, and there were few optional extras. It was reliable and durable, designed to travel effortlessly over dirt roads in rain, snow, or sunshine. It was easy to use and fix. People could learn to drive it in a day. And like Cirque, Ford went outside the industry for a price point, looking at horse-drawn carriages ($400), not other autos. In 1908, the first Model T cost $850; in 1909, the price dropped to $609, and by 1924 it was down to $290. In this way, Ford converted buyers of horse-drawn carriages into car buyers—just as Cirque turned theater-goers into circusgoers. Sales of the Model T boomed. Ford's market share surged from 9% in 1908 to 61% in 1921, and by 1923, a majority of American households had a car.

Even as Ford offered the mass of buyers a leap in value, the company also achieved the lowest cost structure in the industry, much as Cirque did later. By keeping the cars highly standard-ized with limited options and interchangeable parts, Ford was able to scrap the prevailing manufacturing system in which cars were constructed by skilled craftsmen who swarmed around one workstation and built a car piece by piece from start to finish. Ford's revolutionary assembly line replaced craftsmen with unskilled laborers, each of whom worked quickly and efficiently on one small task. This allowed Ford to make a car in just four days—21 days was the industry norm—creating huge cost savings.

Blue and red oceans have always coexisted and always will. Practical reality, therefore, demands that companies understand the strategic logic of both types of oceans. At present, competing in red oceans dominates the field of strategy in theory and in practice, even as businesses' need to create blue oceans intensifies. It is time to even the scales in the field of strategy with a better balance of efforts across both oceans. For although blue ocean strategists have always existed, for the most part their strategies have been largely unconscious. But once corporations realize that the strategies for creating and capturing blue oceans have a different underlying logic from red ocean strategies, they will be able to create many more blue oceans in the future.

TABLE 1

A snapshot of blue ocean creation

This table identifies the strategic elements that were common to blue ocean creations in three different industries in different eras. It is not intended to be comprehensive in coverage or exhaustive in content. We chose to show American industries because they represented the largest and least-regulated market during our study period. The pattern of blue ocean creations exemplified by these three industries is consistent with what we observed in the other industries in our study.

Key blue ocean creations	Was the blue ocean created by a new entrant or an incumbent?	Was it driven by technology pioneering or value pioneering?	At the time of the blue ocean creation, was the industry attractive or unattractive?
Automobiles			
Ford Model T Unveiled in 1908, the Model T was the first mass-produced car, priced so that many Americans could afford it.	New entrant	Value pioneering* (mostly existing technologies)	Unattractive

GM's "car for every purse and purpose" GM created a blue ocean in 1924 by injecting fun and fashion into the car.	Incumbent	Value pioneering (some new technologies)	Attractive
Japanese fuel-efficient autos Japanese automakers created a blue ocean in the mid-1970s with small, reliable lines of cars.	Incumbent	Value pioneering (some new technologies)	Unattractive
Chrysler minivan With its 1984 minivan, Chrysler created a new class of automobile that was as easy to use as a car but had the passenger space of a van.	Incumbent	Value pioneering (mostly existing technologies)	Unattractive

*Driven by value pioneering does not mean that technologies were not involved. Rather, it means that the defining technologies used had largely been in existence, whether in that industry or elsewhere.

(continued)

Key blue ocean creations	Was the blue ocean created by a new entrant or an incumbent?	Was it driven by technology pioneering or value pioneering?	At the time of the blue ocean creation, was the industry attractive or unattractive?
Computers			
CTR's tabulating machine In 1914, CTR created the business machine industry by simplifying, modularizing, and leasing tabulating machines. CTR later changed its name to IBM.	Incumbent	Value pioneering (some new technologies)	Unattractive
IBM 650 electronic computer and System/360 In 1952, IBM created the business computer industry by simplifying and reducing the power and price of existing technology. And it exploded the blue ocean created by the 650 when in 1964 it unveiled the System/360, the first modularized computer system.	Incumbent	Value pioneering (650: mostly existing technologies) Value and technology pioneering (System/360: new and existing technologies)	Nonexistent

		Value pioneering (mostly existing technologies)	
Apple personal computer Although it was not the first home computer, the all-in-one, simple-to-use Apple II was a blue ocean creation when it appeared in 1978.	New entrant	Value pioneering (mostly existing technologies)	Unattractive
Compaq PC servers Compaq created a blue ocean in 1992 with its ProSignia server, which gave buyers twice the file and print capability of the minicomputer at one-third the price.	Incumbent	Value pioneering (mostly existing technologies)	Nonexistent
Dell built-to-order computers In the mid-1990s, Dell created a blue ocean in a highly competitive industry by creating a new purchase and delivery experience for buyers.	New entrant	Value pioneering (mostly existing technologies)	Unattractive
Movie theaters			
Nickelodeon The first Nickelodeon opened its doors in 1905, showing short films around-the-clock to working-class audiences for five cents.	New entrant	Value pioneering (mostly existing technologies)	Nonexistent

(continued)

Key blue ocean creations	Was the blue ocean created by a new entrant or an incumbent?	Was it driven by technology pioneering or value pioneering?	At the time of the blue ocean creation, was the industry attractive or unattractive?
Movie theaters			
Palace theaters Created by Roxy Rothapfel in 1914, these theaters provided an operalike environment for cinema viewing at an affordable price.	Incumbent	Value pioneering (mostly existing technologies)	Attractive
AMC multiplex In the 1960s, the number of multiplexes in America's suburban shopping malls mushroomed. The multiplex gave viewers greater choice while reducing owners' costs.	Incumbent	Value pioneering (mostly existing technologies)	Unattractive
AMC megaplex Megaplexes, introduced in 1995, offered every current blockbuster and provided spectacular viewing experiences in theater complexes as big as stadiums, at a lower cost to theater owners.	Incumbent	Value pioneering (mostly existing technologies)	Unattractive

TABLE 2

Red ocean versus blue ocean strategy

The imperatives for red ocean and blue ocean strategies are starkly different.

Red ocean strategy	Blue ocean strategy
Compete in existing market space.	Create uncontested market space.
Beat the competition.	Make the competition irrelevant.
Exploit existing demand.	Create and capture new demand.
Make the value/cost trade-off.	Break the value/cost trade-off.
Align the whole system of a company's activities with its strategic choice of differentiation *or* low cost.	Align the whole system of a company's activities in pursuit of differentiation *and* low cost.

The simultaneous pursuit of differentiation and low cost

A blue ocean is created in the region where a company's actions favorably affect both its cost structure and its value proposition to buyers. Cost savings are made from eliminating and reducing the factors an industry competes on. Buyer value is lifted by raising and creating elements the industry has never offered. Over time, costs are reduced further as scale economies kick in, due to the high sales volumes that superior value generates.

Article Summary

Idea in Brief

The best way to drive profitable growth? Stop competing in overcrowded industries. In those **red oceans,** companies try to outperform rivals to grab bigger slices of existing demand. As the space gets increasingly crowded, profit and growth prospects shrink. Products become commoditized. Ever-more-intense competition turns the water bloody.

How to avoid the fray? Kim and Mauborgne recommend creating **blue oceans**—uncontested market spaces where the competition is irrelevant. In blue oceans, you invent and capture new demand, and you offer customers a leap in value while also streamlining your costs. Results? Handsome profits, speedy growth—and brand equity that lasts for decades while rivals scramble to catch up.

Consider Cirque du Soleil—which invented a new industry that combined elements from traditional circus with elements drawn from sophisticated theater. In just 20 years, Cirque raked in revenues that Ringling Bros. and Barnum & Bailey—the world's leading circus—needed more than a century to attain.

Red Ocean Traps

In America, corporate performance has been deteriorating for decades. According to Deloitte's landmark study "The Shift Index," the aggregate return on assets of U.S. public companies has fallen below 1%, to about a quarter of its 1965 level. As market power has moved from companies to consumers, and global competition has intensified, managers in almost all industries have come to face steep performance challenges. To turn things around, they need to be more creative in developing and executing their competitive strategies. But long-term success will not be achieved through competitiveness alone. Increasingly, it will depend on the ability to generate new demand and create and capture new markets.

The payoffs of market creation are huge. Just compare the experiences of Apple and Microsoft. Over the past 15 years, Apple has made a series of successful market-creating moves, introducing the iPod, iTunes, the iPhone, the App Store, and the iPad. From the launch of the iPod in 2001 to the end of its 2014 fiscal year, Apple's market cap surged more than 75-fold as its sales and profits exploded. Over the same period,

Microsoft's market cap crept up by a mere 3% while its revenue went from nearly five times larger than Apple's to nearly half of Apple's. With close to 80% of profits coming from two old businesses—Windows and Office—and no compelling market-creating move, Microsoft has paid a steep price.

Of course, it's not that companies don't recognize the value of new market spaces. To the contrary, their leaders increasingly are committed to creating them and dedicate significant amounts of money to efforts to do so. But despite this, few companies seem to crack the code. What, exactly, is getting in their way?

In the decade since the publication of the first edition of our book, *Blue Ocean*

Strategy, we've had conversations with many managers involved in executing market-creating strategies. As they shared their successes and failures with us, we identified a common factor that seemed to consistently undermine their efforts: their mental models—ingrained assumptions and theories about the way the world works. Though mental models lie below people's cognitive awareness, they're so powerful a determinant of choices and behaviors that many neuroscientists think of them almost as automated algorithms that dictate how people respond to changes and events.

Mental models have their merits. In dangerous times, a robust mental model can help you quickly make decisions that are critical to survival. And we have no issue with the soundness of the mental models that we saw managers apply. They were grounded in knowledge acquired in classrooms and from years of business experience. They help managers respond better to competitive challenges. But our conversations suggest that the mental models managers rely on to negotiate existing market spaces also undermine their ability to create new markets.

In our research and discussions, we've encountered six especially salient assumptions built into managers' mental models. We have come to think of them as red ocean traps, because they effectively anchor managers in red oceans—crowded market spaces where companies engage in bloody competition for market share—and prevent them from entering blue oceans, previously unknown and uncontested market spaces with ample potential.

The first two traps stem from assumptions about marketing, in particular an emphasis on customer orientation and niches; the next two from economic lessons on technology innovation and creative destruction; and the final two from principles of competitive strategy that regard differentiation and low cost as mutually exclusive choices. In the following pages, we'll look at each trap in detail and see how it thwarts companies' attempts to create markets.

TRAP ONE: SEEING MARKET-CREATING STRATEGIES AS CUSTOMER-ORIENTED APPROACHES

Generating new demand is at the heart of market-creating strategies. It hinges on converting noncustomers into customers, as Salesforce.com did with its on-demand CRM software, which opened up a new market space by winning over small and midsize firms that had previously rejected CRM enterprise software.

The trouble is that managers, especially those in marketing, have been quite reasonably brought up to believe that the customer is king. It's all too easy for them to assume, therefore, that market-creating strategies are customer led, which causes them to reflexively stick to their focus on existing customers and how to make them happier.

This approach, however, is unlikely to create new markets. To do that, an organization needs to turn its focus to noncustomers and why they refuse to patronize an industry's offering. Noncustomers, not customers, hold the greatest insight into the points of pain and intimidation that limit the boundary of an industry. A focus on existing customers, by contrast, tends to drive organizations to come up with better solutions for them than what competitors currently offer—but keeps companies moored in red oceans.

Consider Sony's launch of the Portable Reader System (PRS) in 2006. The company's aim was to unlock a new market space in books by opening the e-reader market to a wide customer base. To figure out how to realize that goal, it looked to the experience of existing e-reader customers, who were dissatisfied with the size and poor display quality of current products. Sony's response was a thin, lightweight device with an easy-to-read screen. Despite the media's praise and happier customers, the PRS lost out to Amazon's Kindle because it failed to attract the mass of noncustomers whose main reason for rejecting e-readers was the shortage of worthwhile books, not the size and the display of the devices. Without a rich choice of titles and an easy way to download them, the noncustomers stuck to print books.

Amazon understood this when it launched the Kindle in 2007, offering more than four times the number of e-titles available from the PRS and making them easily downloadable over Wi-Fi. Within six hours of their release, Kindles sold out, as print book customers rapidly became e-reader customers as well. Though Sony has since exited e-readers, the Kindle grew the industry from around a mere 2% of total book buyers in 2008 to 28% in 2014. It now offers more than 2.5 million e-titles.

TRAP TWO: TREATING MARKET-CREATING STRATEGIES AS NICHE STRATEGIES

The field of marketing has placed great emphasis on using ever finer market segmentation to identify and capture niche markets. Though niche strategies can often be very effective, uncovering a niche in an existing space is not the same thing as identifying a new market space.

Consider Song, an airline launched in 2003 by Delta. Delta's aim was to create a new market space in low-cost carriers by targeting a distinct segment of fliers. It decided to focus on stylish professional women travelers, a segment it figured had needs and preferences different from those of the businessmen and other passengers most airlines targeted. No airline had ever been built around this group. After many focus group discussions with upwardly mobile and professional women, Delta came up with a plan to cater to them with organic food, custom cocktails, a variety of entertainment choices, free in-flight workouts with complementary exercise bands, and crew members dressed in Kate Spade. The strategy was intended to fill a gap in the market. It may well have done that successfully, but the segment proved too small to be sustainable despite competitive pricing. Song flew its last flight in April 2006, just 36 months after its launch.

Successful market-creating strategies don't focus on finer segmentation. More often, they "desegment" markets by identifying key commonalities across buyer groups that could help generate broader demand. Pret A Manger, a British food chain, looked across three different prepared-lunch buyer groups: restaurant-going professionals, fast food customers, and the brown bag set. Although there were plenty of differences across these groups, there were three key commonalities: All of them wanted a lunch that was fresh and healthful, wanted it fast, and wanted it at a reasonable price. That insight helped Pret A Manger see how it could unlock and aggregate untapped demand across those groups to create a commercially compelling new market.

Its concept was to offer restaurant-quality sandwiches made fresh every day from high-end ingredients, preparing them at a speed even greater than that of fast food, and delivering that experience in a sleek setting at reasonable prices. Today, nearly 30 years on, Pret A Manger continues to enjoy robust profitable growth in the new market space it established.

TRAP THREE: CONFUSING TECHNOLOGY INNOVATION WITH MARKET-CREATING STRATEGIES

R&D and technology innovation are widely recognized as key drivers of market development and industry growth. It's

understandable, therefore, that managers
might assume that they are also key drivers in
the discovery of new markets. But the reality
is that market creation is not inevitably
about technological innovation. Yellow Tail
opened a new market (in its case, for a fun
and simple wine for everyone) without any
bleeding-edge technologies. So did the
coffee chain Starbucks and the performing
arts company Cirque du Soleil. Even when
technology is heavily involved, as it was with
market creators Salesforce.com, Intuit's
Quicken, or Uber, it is not the reason that
new offerings are successful. Such products
and services succeed because they are so
simple to use, fun, and productive that people fall in love with them. The technology

that enables them essentially disappears from buyers' minds.

Consider the Segway Personal Transporter, which was launched in 2001. Was it a technology innovation? Sure. It was the world's first self-balancing human transporter, and it worked well. Lean forward and you go forward; lean back and you go back. This engineering marvel was one of the most-talked-about technology innovations of its time. But most people were unwilling to pay up to $5,000 for a product that posed difficulties in use and convenience: Where could you park it? How would you take it with you in a car? Where could you use it—sidewalks or roads? Could you take it on a bus or a train? Although the Segway was expected to reach breakeven just

six months after its launch, sales fell way below
initial predictions, and the company was sold
in 2009. Not everyone was surprised. At the
time of the product's release, a prescient *Time*
magazine article about Dean Kamen, Segway's
inventor, struck a cautionary note: "One of
the hardest truths for any technologist to hear
is that success or failure in business is rarely
determined by the quality of the technology."

Value innovation, not technology
innovation, is what launches commercially
compelling new markets. Successful new
products or services open market spaces
by offering a leap in productivity, sim-
plicity, ease of use, convenience, fun, or
environmental friendliness. But when companies mistakenly assume that market creation

hinges on breakthrough technologies, their organizations tend to push for products or services that are too "out there," too complicated, or, like the Segway, lacking a necessary ecosystem. In fact, many technology innovations fail to create new markets even if they win the company accolades and their developers scientific prizes.

TRAP FOUR: EQUATING CREATIVE DESTRUCTION WITH MARKET CREATION

Joseph Schumpeter's theory of creative destruction lies at the heart of innovation economics. Creative destruction occurs when an invention disrupts a market by displacing an earlier technology or existing product or service. Digital photography, for example, wiped out the photographic film industry, becoming the new norm. In Schumpeter's framework, the old is incessantly destroyed and replaced by the new.

But does market creation always involve destruction? The answer is no. It also involves nondestructive creation, wherein new demand is created without displacing existing products or services. Take Viagra, which established a new market in lifestyle drugs. Did Viagra make any earlier technology or existing product or service obsolete? No. It unlocked new demand by offering for the first time a real solution to a major problem experienced by many men in their personal relationships. Grameen Bank's creation of the microfinance industry is another example. Many market-creating moves are nondestructive, because they offer solutions where none previously existed. We've also seen this happen with the social networking and crowdfunding industries. And even when a certain amount of destruction is involved in market creation, nondestructive creation is often a larger element than you might think. Nintendo's Wii game player, for example, complemented more than replaced existing game systems, because it attracted younger children and older adults who hadn't previously played video games.

Conflating market creation with creative destruction not only limits an organization's set of opportunities but also sets off resistance to market-creating strategies. People in established companies typically don't like the notion of creative destruction or disruption because it may threaten their current status and jobs. As a result, managers often undermine their company's market-creating efforts by starving them of resources, allocating undue overhead costs to the initiatives, or not cooperating with the people working on them. It's critical for market creators to head this danger off early by clarifying that their project is at least as much about nondestructive creation as it is about disruption.

TRAP FIVE: EQUATING MARKET-CREATING STRATEGIES WITH DIFFERENTIATION

In a competitive industry companies tend to choose their position on what economists call the "productivity frontier," the range of value-cost trade-offs that are available given the structure and norms of the industry. Differentiation is the strategic position on this frontier in which a company stands out from competitors by providing premium value; the trade-off is usually higher costs to the company and higher prices for customers. We've found that many managers assume that market creation is the same thing.

In reality, a market-creating move breaks the value-cost trade-off. It is about pursuing differentiation and low cost simultaneously. Are Yellow Tail and Salesforce.com differentiated from other players? You bet. But are Yellow Tail and Salesforce.com also low cost? Yes again. A market-creating move is a "both-and," not an "either-or," strategy. It's important to realize this difference, because when companies mistakenly assume that market creation is synonymous with differentiation, they often focus on what to improve or create to stand apart and pay scant heed to what they can eliminate or reduce to simultaneously achieve low cost. As a result, they may inadvertently become premium competitors in an existing industry space rather than discover a new market space of their own.

Take BMW, which set out to establish a new market in urban transport with its launch of the C1 in 2000. Traffic problems in European cities are severe, and people waste many hours commuting by car there, so BMW wanted to develop a vehicle people could use to beat rush-hour congestion. The C1 was a two-wheeled scooter targeting the premium end of the market. Unlike other scooters, it had a roof and a full windshield with wipers. BMW also invested heavily in safety. The C1 held drivers in place with a four-point seat-belt system and protected them with an aluminum roll cage, two shoulder-height roll bars, and a crumple zone around the front wheel.

With all these extra features, the C1 was expensive to build, and its price ranged from

$7,000 to $10,000–far more than the $3,000 to $5,000 that typical scooters fetched. Although the C1 succeeded in differentiating itself within the scooter industry, it did not create the new market space in transportation BMW had hoped for. In the summer of 2003, BMW announced it was stopping production because the C1 hadn't met sales expectations.

TRAP SIX: EQUATING MARKET-CREATING STRATEGIES WITH LOW-COST STRATEGIES

This trap, in which managers assume that they can create a new market solely by driving down costs, is the obvious flip side of trap five. When organizations see market-creating strategies as synonymous with low-cost strategies alone, they focus on what to eliminate and reduce in current offerings and largely ignore what they should improve or create to increase the offerings' value.

Ouya is a video-game console maker that fell into this trap. When the company began selling its products, in June 2013, big players like Sony, Microsoft, and Nintendo were offering consoles connected to TV screens and controllers that provided a high-quality gaming experience, for prices ranging from $199 to $419. With no low-cost console available, many people would play video games either on handheld devices or on TV screens connected to mobile devices via inexpensive cables.

An attempt to create a market space between high-end consoles and mobile handhelds, the $99 Ouya was introduced as a low-cost open-source "microconsole" offering reasonable quality on TV screens and most games free to try. Although people admired the inexpensive, simple device, Ouya didn't have the rich catalog of quality games, 3-D intensity, great graphics, and processing speed that traditional gamers prized but the company had to some extent sacrificed to drop cost and price. At the same time, Ouya lacked the distinctive advantage of mobile handheld devices—namely, their play-on-the-go functionality. In the absence of those features, potential gamers had no compelling reason to buy

Ouyas. The company is now shopping itself to acquirers—on the basis of its staff's talent more than the strength of its console business—but as yet hasn't found one.

Our point, again, is that a market-creating strategy takes a "both-and" approach: It pursues both differentiation and low cost. In this framework, new market space is created not by pricing against the competition within an industry but by pricing against substitutes and alternatives that noncustomers are currently using. Accordingly, a new market does not have to be created at the low end of an industry. Instead it can be created at the high end, as Cirque du Soleil did in circus entertainment, Starbucks did in coffee, and Dyson did in vacuum cleaners.

Even when companies create new markets at the low end, the offerings also are clearly differentiated in the eyes of buyers. Consider Southwest Airlines and Swatch. Southwest stands out for its friendly, fast, ground-transportation-in-the-air feel, while stylish, fun designs make Swatches a fashion statement. Both companies' offerings are perceived as both differentiated and low cost.

The approaches or strategies presented as the red ocean traps are not wrong or bad. They all serve important purposes. A customer focus, for example, can improve products and services, and technology innovation is a key input for market development and economic growth. Likewise, differentiation or low cost is an effective competitive strategy. What these approaches are not, however, is the path to successful market-creating strategies. And when they drive market-creating efforts that involve big investments, they may result in new businesses that don't earn back those investments and that ultimately fail, as we have seen here. That's why it's key to surface and check the mental models and assumptions of the people who are central to executing market-creating strategies. If those models and assumptions are misaligned with the intended strategic purpose of new market creation, you need to challenge, question, and reframe them. Otherwise, you may fall into the red ocean traps.

Article Summary

Idea in Brief

The Problem

To succeed in the long term, companies must find ways to create new markets. Competing in existing markets is growing less profitable. But despite much investment and commitment, companies find it extraordinarily difficult to establish new market spaces.

Why It Happens

Managers' mental models are based on their experiences in existing markets. Though these assumptions and beliefs have worked in the past, they undermine efforts to create new spaces.

The Solution

To avoid being trapped in old markets, managers need to:

- focus on attracting new customers

- worry less about segmentation

- understand that market creation is not synonymous with either technological innovation or creative destruction

- stop focusing on premium versus low-cost strategies

Blue Ocean
Leadership

I t's a sad truth about the workplace: just 30% of employees are actively committed to doing a good job. According to Gallup's 2013 *State of the American Workplace* report, 50% of employees merely put their time in, while the remaining 20% act out their discontent in counterproductive ways, negatively influencing their coworkers, missing days on the job, and driving customers away through poor service. Gallup estimates that the 20% group alone costs the

US economy around half a trillion dollars each year.

What's the reason for the widespread employee disengagement? According to Gallup, poor leadership is a key cause.

Most executives—not just those in America—recognize that one of their biggest challenges is closing the vast gulf between the potential and the realized talent and energy of the people they lead. As one CEO put it, "We have a large workforce that has an appetite to do a good job up and down the ranks. If we can transform them—tap into them through effective leadership—there will be an awful lot of people out there doing an awful lot of good."

Of course, managers don't intend to be poor leaders. The problem is that they lack a clear understanding of just what changes it would take to bring out the best in everyone and achieve high impact. We believe that leaders can obtain this understanding through an approach we call "blue ocean leadership." It draws on our research on blue ocean strategy, our model for creating new market space by converting noncustomers into customers, and applies its concepts and analytic frameworks to help leaders release the blue ocean of unexploited talent and energy in their organizations—rapidly and at low cost.

The underlying insight is that leadership, in essence, can be thought of as a service that people in an organization "buy" or "don't buy." Every leader in that sense has customers: the bosses to whom the leader must deliver performance, and the followers who need the leader's guidance and support to achieve. When people value your leadership practices, they in effect buy your leadership. They're inspired to excel and act with commitment. But when employees don't buy your leadership, they disengage, becoming noncustomers of your leadership. Once we started thinking about leadership in this way, we began to see that the concepts and frameworks we were developing to create new demand by converting noncustomers into customers could be adapted to help leaders convert disengaged employees into engaged ones.

Over the past 10 years we and Gavin Fraser, a Blue Ocean Strategy Network expert, have interviewed hundreds of people in organizations to understand where leadership was falling short and how it could be transformed while conserving leaders' most precious resource: time. In this article we present the results of our research.

KEY DIFFERENCES FROM CONVENTIONAL LEADERSHIP APPROACHES

Blue ocean leadership rapidly brings about a step change in leadership strength. It's distinct from traditional leadership development approaches in several overarching ways. Here are the three most salient:

Focus on acts and activities

Over many years a great deal of research has generated insights into the values, qualities, and behavioral styles that make for good leadership, and these have formed the basis of development programs and executive coaching. The implicit assumption is that changes in values, qualities, and behavioral styles ultimately translate into high performance.

But when people look back on these programs, many struggle to find evidence of notable change. As one executive put it, "Without years of dedicated efforts, how can you transform a person's character or behavioral traits? And can you really measure and assess whether leaders are embracing and internalizing these personal traits and styles? In theory, yes, but in reality it's hard at best."

Blue ocean leadership, by contrast, focuses on *what acts and activities leaders need to undertake* to boost their teams' motivation and business results, not on *who leaders need to be*. This difference in emphasis is important.

It is markedly easier to change people's acts and activities than their values, qualities, and behavioral traits. Of course, altering a leader's activities is not a complete solution, and having the right values, qualities, and behavioral traits matters. But activities are something that any individual can change, given the right feedback and guidance.

Connect closely to market realities

Traditional leadership development programs tend to be quite generic and are often detached from what firms stand for in the eyes of customers and from the market results people are expected to achieve. In contrast, under blue ocean leadership, the people who face market realities are asked for their direct input on how their leaders hold them back and what those leaders could do to help them best serve customers and other key stakeholders. And when people are engaged in defining the leadership practices that will enable them to thrive, and *those practices are connected to the market realities* against which they need to perform, they're highly motivated to create the best possible profile for leaders and to make the new solutions work. Their willing cooperation maximizes the acceptance of new profiles for leadership while minimizing implementation costs.

Distribute leadership across all management levels

Most leadership programs focus on executives and their potential for impact now and in the future. But the key to a successful organization is having empowered leaders at every level, because outstanding organizational performance often comes down to the motivation and actions of middle and frontline leaders, who are in closer contact with the market. As one senior executive put it, "The truth is that we, the top management, are not in the field to fully appreciate the middle and frontline actions. We need effective leaders at every level to maximize corporate performance."

Blue ocean leadership is designed to be applied across the three distinct management levels: *top, middle*, and *frontline*. It calls for profiles for leaders that are tailored to the very different tasks, degrees of power, and environments you find at each level. Extending leadership capabilities deep into the front line unleashes the latent talent and drive of a critical mass of employees, and creating strong distributed leadership significantly enhances performance across the organization.

THE FOUR STEPS OF BLUE OCEAN LEADERSHIP

Now let's walk through how to put blue ocean leadership into practice. It involves four steps.

1. See your leadership reality

A common mistake organizations make is to discuss changes in leadership before resolving differences of opinion over what leaders are actually doing. Without a common understanding of where leadership stands and is falling short, a forceful case for change cannot be made.

Achieving this understanding is the objective of the first step. It takes the form of what we call as-is Leadership Canvases, analytic visuals that show just how managers at each level invest their time and effort, as perceived by the customers of their leadership. An organization begins the process by creating a canvas for each of its three management levels.

A team of 12 to 15 senior managers is typically selected to carry out this project. The people chosen should cut across functions and be recognized as good leaders in the company so that the team has immediate credibility. The team is then broken into three smaller subteams, each focused on one level and charged with interviewing its relevant leadership customers—both bosses and subordinates—and ensuring that a representative number of each are included.

The aim is to uncover how people experience current leadership and to start a companywide conversation about what leaders do and should do at each level. The customers of leaders are asked which acts and activities—good and bad—their leaders spend most of their time on, and which are key to motivation and performance but are neglected by their leaders. Getting at the specifics is important; the as-is canvases must be grounded in acts and activities that reflect each level's specific market reality and performance goals. This involves a certain amount of probing.

At a company we'll call British Retail Group (BRG), many interviewees commented that middle managers spent much of their time playing politics. The subteam focused on that level pushed for clarification and discovered that two acts principally accounted for this judgment. One was that the leaders tended to divide responsibility among people, which created uncertainty about accountability—and some internal competitiveness. The result was a lot of finger-pointing and the perception that the leaders were playing people against one another. The subteam also found that the leaders spent much of their time in meetings with senior management. This led subordinates to conclude that their leaders were more interested in maximizing political "face time" and spinning news than in being present to support them.

After four to six weeks of interviews, subteam members come together to create as-is Leadership Profiles by pooling their findings and determining, based on frequency of citation, the dominant leadership acts and activities at each level. To help the subteams focus on what really matters, we typically ask for no more than 10 to 15 leadership acts and activities per level. These get registered on the horizontal axis of the as-is canvas, and the extent to which leaders do them is registered on the vertical axis. The cap of 10 to 15 prevents the canvas from becoming a statement of everything and nothing.

The result is almost always eye-opening. It's not uncommon to find that 20% to 40% of the acts and activities of leaders at all three levels provide only questionable value to those above and below them. It's also not uncommon to find that leaders are underinvesting in 20% to 40% of the acts and activities that interviewees at their level cite as important.

At BRG, the canvas for senior managers revealed that their customers thought they spent most of their time on essentially middle-management acts and activities, while the canvas of middle managers indicated that they seemed to be absorbed in protecting bureaucratic procedures. Frontline leaders were seen to be focused on trying to keep their bosses happy by doing things like deferring customer queries to them, which satisfied their desire to be in control. When we asked team members to describe each canvas in a tagline, an exercise that's part of the process, they labeled the frontline Leadership Profile "Please the Boss," the middle-manager profile "Control and Play Safe," and the senior manager profile "Focus on the Day-to-Day." (For an example, see the exhibit "What middle managers actually do.")

The implications were depressing. The biggest "aha" for the subteams was that senior managers appeared to have scarcely any time to do the real job of top management—thinking, probing, identifying opportunities on the horizon, and gearing up the organization to capitalize on them. Faced with firsthand, repeated evidence of the shortcomings of leadership practices, the subteams could not defend the current Leadership Profiles. The canvases made a strong case for change at all three levels; it was clear that people throughout the organization wished for it.

2. Develop alternative Leadership Profiles

At this point the subteams are usually eager to explore what effective Leadership Profiles would look like at each level. To achieve this, they go back to their interviewees with two sets of questions.

The first set is aimed at pinpointing the extent to which each act and activity on the canvas is either a cold spot (absorbing leaders' time but adding little or no value) or a hot spot (energizing employees and inspiring them to apply their talents, but currently underinvested in by leaders or not addressed at all).

The second set prompts interviewees to think beyond the bounds of the company and focus on effective leadership acts they've observed outside the organization, in particular those that could have a strong impact if adopted by internal leaders at their level. Here fresh ideas emerge about what leaders could be doing but aren't. This is not, however, about benchmarking against corporate icons; employees' personal experiences are more likely to produce insights. Most of us have come across people in our lives who have had a disproportionately positive influence on us. It might be a sports coach, a schoolteacher, a scoutmaster, a grandparent, or a former boss. Whoever those role models are, it's important to get interviewees to detail which acts and activities they believe would add real value for them if undertaken by their current leaders.

To process the findings from the second round of interviews, the subteams apply an analytic tool we call the Blue Ocean Leadership Grid (see the table by the same name). For each leadership level the interview results get incorporated into this grid. Typically, we start with the cold-spot acts and activities, which go into the Eliminate or Reduce quadrants depending on how negatively interviewees judge them. This energizes the subteams right away, because people immediately perceive the benefits of stopping leaders from doing things that add little or no value. Cutting back on those activities also gives leaders the time and space they need to raise their game. Without that breathing room, a step change in leadership strength would remain largely wishful thinking, given leaders' already full plates. From the cold spots we move to the hot spots, which go into the Raise quadrant if they involve current acts and activities or Create for those not currently performed at all by leaders. With this input, the subteams draft two to four "to-be" canvases for each leadership level. These analytic visuals illustrate Leadership Profiles that can lift individual and organizational performance, and juxtapose them against the as-is Leadership Profiles. The subteams produce a range of leadership models, rather than stop at one set of possibilities, to thoroughly explore new leadership space.

3. Select to-be Leadership Profiles

After two to three weeks of drawing and redrawing their Leadership Canvases, the subteams present them at what we call a "leadership fair." Fair attendees include board members and top, middle, and front-line managers.

The event starts with members of the original senior team behind the effort describing the process and presenting the three as-is canvases. With those three visuals, the team establishes why change is necessary, confirms that comments from interviewees at all levels were taken into account, and sets the context against which the to-be Leadership Profiles can be understood and appreciated. Although the as-is canvases often present a sobering reality, as they did at BRG, the Leadership Profiles are shown and discussed only at the aggregate level. That makes individual leaders more open to change, because they feel that everyone is in the same boat.

With the stage set, the subteams present the to-be profiles, hanging their canvases on the walls so that the audience can easily see them. Typically, the subteam that focused on frontline leaders will go first. After the presentation, the attendees are each given three Post-it notes and told to put one next to their favorite Leadership Profile. And if they find that canvas especially compelling, they can put up to three Post-its on it.

After all the votes are in, the company's senior executives probe the attendees about why they voted as they did. The same process is then repeated for the two other leadership levels. (We find it easier to deal with each level separately and sequentially, and that doing so increases voters' recall of the discussion.)

After about four hours everyone in attendance has a clear picture of the current Leadership Profile of each level, the completed Blue Ocean Leadership Grids, and a selection of to-be Leadership Profiles that could create a significant change in leadership performance. Armed with this information and the votes and comments of attendees, the top managers convene outside the fair room and decide which to-be Leadership Profile to move forward on at each level. Then they return and explain their decisions to the fair's participants.

At BRG, more than 125 people voted on the profiles, and fair attendees greeted the three that were selected with enthusiasm. The tagline for frontline leaders' to-be profile was "Cut Through the Crap." (Sadly, this was later refined to "Cut Through to Serve Customers.") In this profile, frontline leaders did not defer the vast majority of customer queries to middle management and spent less time jumping through procedural hoops. Their time was directed to training frontline personnel to deliver on company promises on the spot, resolve customer problems, quickly help customers in distress, and make meaningful cross-sales—leadership acts and activities that fired up the frontline workers, were sure to excite customers, and would have a direct impact on the company's bottom line.

"Liberate, Coach, and Empower" was the tagline for middle management's to-be profile. Here leaders' time and attention shifted from controlling to supporting employees.

This involved eliminating and reducing a range of oversight activities—such as requiring weekly reports on customer calls received and funds spent on office supplies—that sapped people's energy and kept front-line leaders at their desks. The profile also included new actions aimed at managing, disseminating, and integrating the knowledge of frontline leaders and their staff. In practical terms, this meant spending much more time providing face-to-face coaching and feedback.

The tagline for the to-be profile of senior management was "Delegate and Chart the Company's Future." With the acts and activities of frontline and middle managers reset, senior managers would be freed up to devote a significant portion of their time to thinking about the big picture—the changes in the industry and their implications for strategy and the organization. They would spend less time putting out fires.

The board members who attended the leadership fair felt strongly that the to-be Leadership Profiles supported the interests of customers as well as shareholders' profit and growth objectives. The frontline leaders were energized and ready to charge ahead. Senior managers went from feeling towed under the waves by all the middle management duties they had to coordinate and attend to, to feeling as if they could finally get their heads above water and see the beauty of the ocean they had to chart.

The trickiest to-be Leadership Profile was middle management's. Letting go of control and empowering the people below them can be tough for folks in this organizational tier. But the to-be Leadership Profiles of both frontline and senior management helped clear the path to change at this level.

4. Institutionalize new leadership practices

After the fair is over, the original subteam members communicate the results to the people they interviewed who were not at the fair.

Organizations then distribute the agreed-on to-be profiles to the leaders at each level. The subteam members hold meetings with leaders to walk them through their canvases, explaining what should be eliminated, reduced, raised, and created. This step reinforces the buy-in that the initiative has been building by briefing leaders throughout the organization on key findings at each step of the process and tapping many of them for input. And because every leader is in effect the buyer of another level of leadership, all managers will be working to change, knowing that their bosses will be doing the same thing on the basis of input they directly provided.

The leaders are then charged with passing the message along to their direct reports and explaining to them how the new Leadership Profiles will allow them to be more effective. To keep the new profiles top of mind, the to-be canvases are pinned up prominently in the offices of both the leaders and their reports. Leaders are tasked with holding regular monthly meetings at which they gather their direct reports' feedback on how well they're making the transition to the new profiles. All comments must be illustrated with specific examples. Has the leader cut back on the acts and activities that were to be eliminated and reduced in the new Leadership Profile? If yes, how? If not, in what instances was she still engaging in them? Likewise, is she focusing more on what does add value and doing the new activities in her profile? Though the meetings can be unnerving at first—both for employees who have to critique the boss and for the bosses whose actions are being exposed to scrutiny—it doesn't take long before a team spirit and mutual respect take hold, as all people see how the changes in leadership are positively influencing their performance.

Through the changes highlighted by the to-be profiles, BRG was able to deepen its leadership strength and achieve high impact at lower cost. Consider the results produced just at the frontline level: Turnover of BRG's 10,000-plus frontline employees dropped from about 40% to 11% in the first year, reducing both recruitment and training costs by some 50%. The total savings, including those from decreased absenteeism, amounted to more than $50 million that year. On top of that, BRG's customer satisfaction scores climbed by over 30%, and leaders at all levels reported feeling less stressed, more energized by their ability to act, and more confident that they were making a greater contribution to the company, customers, and their own personal development.

EXECUTION IS BUILT INTO THE FOUR STEPS

Any change initiative faces skepticism. Think of it as the "bend over—here it comes again" syndrome. While blue ocean leadership also meets such a reaction initially, it counters it by building good execution into the process. The four steps are founded on the principles of fair process: engagement, explanation, and expectation clarity. The power of these principles cannot be overstated, and we have written extensively about their impact on the quality of execution for over 20 years. (See, for example, our article "Fair Process: Managing in the Knowledge Economy," HBR, July–August 1997.)

In the leadership development context, the application of fair process achieves buy-in and ownership of the to-be Leadership Profiles and builds trust, preparing the ground for implementation. The principles are applied in a number of ways, with the most important practices being:

- *Respected senior managers spearhead the process.* Their engagement is not ceremonial; they conduct interviews and draw the canvases. This strongly signals the importance of the initiative, which makes people at all levels feel respected and gives senior managers a visceral sense of what actions are needed to create a step change in leadership performance. Here's a typical employee reaction: "At first, I thought this was just one of those initiatives where management loves to talk about the need for change but then essentially goes back to doing what they've always done. But when I saw that leading senior managers were driving the process and rolling up their sleeves to push the change, I thought to myself, 'Hmm . . . they may just finally mean it.'"

- *People are engaged in defining what leaders should do.* Since the to-be profiles are generated with the employees' own input, people have confidence in the changes made. The process also makes them feel more deeply engaged with their leaders, because they have greater ownership of what their leaders are doing. Here's what people told us: "Senior management said they were going to come and talk to people at all levels to understand what we need our leaders to do and not do, so we could thrive. And I thought, 'I'll believe it when someone comes knocking on my door.' And then they knocked."

- *People at all levels have a say in the final decision.* A slice of the organization across the three management levels gets to vote in selecting the new Leadership Profiles. Though the top managers have the final say on the to-be profiles and may not choose those with the most votes, they are required to provide a clear, sound explanation for their decisions in front of all attendees. Here's some typical feedback: "The doubts we had that our comments were just paid lip service to were dispelled when we saw how our inputs were figured into the to-be profiles. We realized then that our voices were heard."

- *It's easy to assess whether expectations are being met.* Clarity about what needs to change to move from the as-is to the to-be Leadership Profiles makes it simple to monitor progress. The monthly review meetings between leaders and their direct reports help the organization check whether it's making headway. We've found that those meetings keep leaders honest, motivate them to continue with change, and build confidence in both the process and the sincerity of the leaders. By collecting feedback from those meetings, top management can assess how rapidly leaders are making the shift from their as-is to their to-be Leadership Profiles, which becomes a key input in annual performance evaluations. This is what people say: "With the one-page visual of our old and new Leadership Profiles, we can easily track the progress in moving from the old to the new. In it, everyone can see with clarity precisely where we are in closing the gap."

Essentially, the gift that fair process confers is trust and, hence, voluntary cooperation, a quality vital to the leader-follower relationship. Anyone who has ever worked in an organization understands how important trust is. If you trust the process and the people you work for, you're willing to go the extra mile and give your best. If you don't trust them, you'll stick to the letter of the law that binds your contract with the organization and devote your energy to protecting your position and fighting over turf rather than to winning customers and creating value. Not only will your abilities be wasted, but they will often work against your organization's performance.

BECOMING A BLUE OCEAN LEADER

We never cease to be amazed by the talent and energy we see in the organizations we study. Sadly, we are equally amazed by how much of it is squandered by poor leadership. Blue ocean leadership can help put an end to that.

The Leadership Canvases give people a concrete, visual framework in which they can surface and discuss the improvements leaders need to make. The fairness of the process makes the implementation and monitoring of those changes far easier than in traditional top-down approaches. Moreover, blue ocean leadership achieves a transformation with less time and effort, because leaders are not trying to alter who they are and break the habits of a lifetime. They are simply changing the tasks they carry out. Better yet, one of the strengths of blue ocean leadership is its scalability. You don't have to wait for your company's top leadership to launch this process. Whatever management level you belong to, you can awaken the sleeping potential of your people by taking them through the four steps.

Are you ready to be a blue ocean leader?

TABLE 1

The Blue Ocean Leadership Grid

The Blue Ocean Leadership Grid is an analytic tool that challenges people to think about which acts and activities leaders should do less of because they hold people back, and which leaders should do more of because they inspire people to give their all. Current activities from the leaders' "as-is" profiles (which may add value or not), along with new activities that employees believe would add a lot of value if leaders started doing them, are assigned to the four categories in the grid. Organizations then use the grids to develop new profiles of effective leadership.

Eliminate	Reduce	Raise	Create
What acts and activities do leaders invest their time and intelligence in that should be eliminated?	What acts and activities do leaders invest their time and intelligence in that should be reduced well below their current level?	What acts and activities do leaders invest their time and intelligence in that should be raised well above their current level?	What acts and activities should leaders invest their time and intelligence in that they currently don't undertake?

What middle managers actually do

As-is Leadership Canvases show the activities that employees see leaders engaging in, and the amount of time and energy they think leaders spend on each. The canvas below, for middle managers at the retail company BRG, reveals that people viewed them as rule enforcers who played it safe.

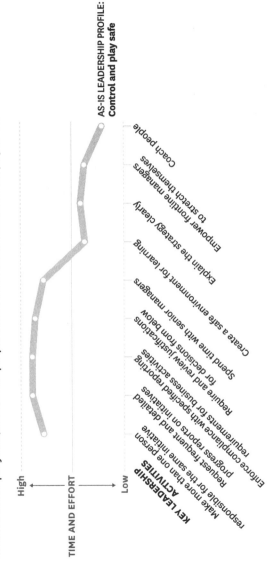

TIME AND EFFORT — High / Low

KEY LEADERSHIP ACTIVITIES

- Make more than one person responsible for the same initiative
- Request frequent and detailed progress reports on initiatives
- Enforce compliance with specified requirements for business activities
- Require and review justifications for decisions from below
- Spend time with senior managers
- Create a safe environment for learning
- Explain the strategy clearly
- Empower frontline managers to stretch themselves
- Coach people

AS-IS LEADERSHIP PROFILE: Control and play safe

To-be Leadership Canvas

Frontline managers: Serve customers, not the boss

Current activities of BRG's frontline leaders vs. the activities employees think they should be doing:

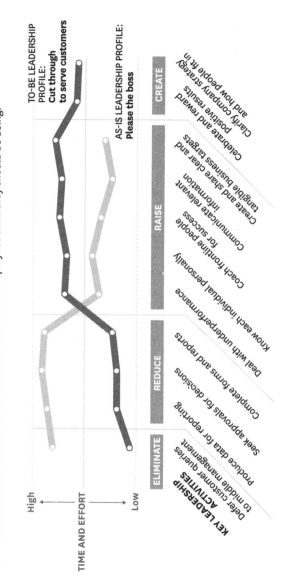

TO-BE LEADERSHIP PROFILE: **Cut through to serve customers**

AS-IS LEADERSHIP PROFILE: **Please the boss**

TIME AND EFFORT — High / Low

KEY LEADERSHIP ACTIVITIES

ELIMINATE
- Defer customer queries to middle management
- Produce data for reporting

REDUCE
- Seek approvals for decisions
- Complete forms and reports
- Deal with underperformance

RAISE
- Know each individual personally
- Coach frontline people
- Communicate relevant information
- Create and share clear and tangible business targets
- Celebrate and reward positive results

CREATE
- Clarify company strategy and how people fit in

To-be Leadership Canvas

Middle managers: More coaching, less control

Current activities of BRG's midlevel leaders vs. the activities employees think they should be doing:

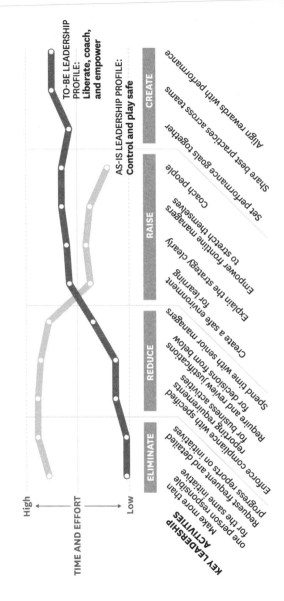

TO-BE LEADERSHIP PROFILE: **Liberate, coach, and empower**

AS-IS LEADERSHIP PROFILE: **Control and play safe**

TIME AND EFFORT — High / Low

ELIMINATE	REDUCE	RAISE	CREATE

KEY LEADERSHIP ACTIVITIES

- Make more than one person responsible for the same initiative
- Request frequent progress reports on initiatives
- Enforce compliance with specified reporting requirements for business activities
- Require and review justifications for decisions from below
- Spend time with senior managers
- Create a safe environment for learning
- Explain the strategy clearly
- Empower frontline managers to stretch themselves
- Coach people
- Set performance goals together
- Share best practices across teams
- Align rewards with performance

To-be Leadership Canvas

Senior managers: From the day-to-day to the big picture

Current activities of BRG's senior managers vs. the activities employees think they should be doing:

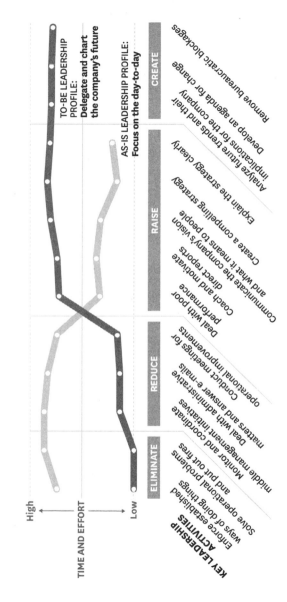

TIME AND EFFORT — High / Low

TO-BE LEADERSHIP PROFILE: Delegate and chart the company's future

AS-IS LEADERSHIP PROFILE: Focus on the day-to-day

KEY LEADERSHIP ACTIVITIES

ELIMINATE
- Enforce established ways of doing things
- Solve operational problems and put out fires
- Monitor and coordinate middle management initiatives

REDUCE
- Deal with administrative matters and answer e-mails
- Conduct meetings for operational improvements

RAISE
- Deal with poor performance
- Coach and motivate direct reports
- Communicate the company's vision and what it means to people
- Create a compelling strategy
- Explain the strategy clearly

CREATE
- Analyze future trends and their implications for the company
- Develop an agenda for change
- Remove bureaucratic blockages

Article Summary

Idea in Brief

The Problem

According to Gallup, only 30% of employees actively apply their talent and energy to move their organizations forward. Fifty percent are just putting their time in, while the remaining 20% act out their discontent in counterproductive ways. Gallup estimates that the 20% group alone costs the US economy around half a trillion dollars each year. A main cause of employee disengagement is poor leadership, Gallup says.

The Solution

A new approach called blue ocean leadership can release the sea of unexploited talent and energy in organizations. It involves a four-step process that allows leaders to gain a clear understanding of just what changes it would take to bring out the best in their people, while conserving their most precious resource: time. An analytic tool, the Leadership Canvas, shows leaders what activities they need to eliminate, reduce, raise, and create to convert disengaged employees into engaged ones.

Case in Point

A British retail group applied blue ocean leadership to redefine what effectiveness meant for frontline, midlevel, and senior leaders. The impact was significant. On the front line, for example, employee turnover dropped from about 40% to 11% in the first year, reducing recruitment and training costs by 50%. Factoring in reduced absenteeism, the group saved more than $50 million in the first year, while customer satisfaction scores climbed by over 30%.

INDEX

Index

Index

Index

Index

Index

Index

ABOUT THE AUTHORS

W. Chan Kim and *Renée Mauborgne* are professors of strategy at INSEAD and codirectors of the INSEAD Blue Ocean Strategy Institute. They are the authors of the *New York Times* and #1 *Wall Street Journal* bestseller, *Blue Ocean Shift* and the international bestseller *Blue Ocean Strategy,* which is recognized as one of the most iconic and impactful strategy books ever written. *Blue Ocean Strategy* has sold over 3.6 million copies, is being published in a record-breaking 46 languages, and is a bestseller across five continents. Kim and Mauborgne rank in the top five management gurus in the world in the Thinkers50 list, a title they have held for ten straight years, and are the recipients of numerous academic and management awards around the world, including the Nobels Colloquia Prize for Leadership on Business and Economic Thinking, the Carl S. Sloane Award by the Association of Management Consulting Firms, the Leadership Hall of Fame by *Fast Company,* and the Eldridge Haynes Prize by the Academy of International Business, among others. They are Fellows of the World Economic Forum and the founders of the Blue Ocean Global Network. For more on these authors and their new book, *Blue Ocean Shift,* see www.blueoceanstrategy.com.

CREATE UNCONTESTED MARKET SPACE AND MAKE THE COMPETITION IRRELEVANT

If you enjoyed reading *Blue Ocean Classics*, turn to this expanded edition of the landmark bestseller, *Blue Ocean Strategy* embraced by business leaders and organizations worldwide.

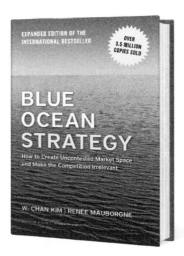

hbr.org/books

The most important management ideas all in one place.

We hope you enjoyed this book from *Harvard Business Review*. For the best ideas HBR has to offer turn to HBR's 10 Must Reads Boxed Set. From books on leadership and strategy to managing yourself and others, this 6-book collection delivers articles on the most essential business topics to help you succeed.

HBR's 10 Must Reads Series

The definitive collection of ideas and best practices on our most sought-after topics from the best minds in business.

- Change Management
- Collaboration
- Communication
- Emotional Intelligence
- Innovation
- Leadership
- Making Smart Decisions

- Managing Across Cultures
- Managing People
- Managing Yourself
- Strategic Marketing
- Strategy
- Teams
- The Essentials

hbr.org/mustreads